A Young Vic/Théâtre de la Ville-Paris co-production, ~~
Nuits de Fourvière/Département du Rhône, Festival Grec 2011 – Barcelona and Festival d'Avignon

By JON FOSSE
English language version by SIMON STEPHENS

This production of *I Am the Wind* was first performed at the Young Vic in May 2011.

I AM THE WIND

by Jon Fosse
English language version by Simon Stephens

The One **Tom Brooke**
The Other **Jack Laskey**

Direction **Patrice Chéreau**
Artistic Collaboration **Thierry Thieû Niang**
Set **Richard Peduzzi**
Costumes **Caroline de Vivaise**
Light **Dominique Bruguière**
Music **Éric Neveux**

Casting **Sam Jones CDG**
Assistant Lighting Design **François Thouret**
Assistant Direction **Peter Cant**
Literal Translation **Øystein Ulsberg Brager**
Design Assistant **Clemence Bezat**
Design Assistant **Bernard Giraud**

Stage Manager **Hazel Price**
Deputy Stage Manager **Amy Almond**
Technical Assistant Stage Manager **Mark Richards**
Costume Supervisor **Catherine Kodicek**
Associate Costume Supervisor **Jo Green**
Touring Production Electrician **Joe Hicks**

Scenic Art **Richard Nutbourne Scenic Studio**
Set and Engineering **Weldfab Stage Engineering Limited**
Water Consultants **Water Sculptures**
Additional set built in the Young Vic workshops.

With very special thanks to Hub Stoke Newington – hubshop.co.uk, and Tony at Reiss.

 Lead sponsor of the **Young Vic's Funded Ticket Scheme**

SUBSIDISED REHEARSAL FACILITIES PROVIDED BY
 JERWOOD **SPACE**

Le vent menaçait, il s'est levé soudain. Ils sont deux sur un fragile bateau: une promenade en mer, un arrêt dans une crique, un verre de schnaps, un peu de nourriture. Et voici que l'un d'eux décide de pousser plus loin, vers la haute mer.

Et nous sommes en haute mer – déjà cela: figurer sur une scène de théâtre le voyage, le trajet, les îles au large, le brouillard et l'océan, calme et bientôt menaçant. Figurer dans un même mouvement la traversée du chenal et l'ombre de la dépression maintenue à distance et qui revient à toute force; la fraternité – l'amour? – qui devient peu à peu intenable, de si peu de poids, jusqu'à l'accident final qui apportera le calme et la paix et paradoxalement la légèreté enfin.

Un voyage à l'intérieur de deux vies entremêlées, une odyssée.

The wind had been threatening. Suddenly, it picked up. There were two of them in a delicate boat: rowing along, stopping off in a cove, a glass of schnapps, a bite to eat. Then one decides to push on further, out into the open sea.

And we are on the open sea... just like that: creating on a stage the journey, the distance travelled, the far away islands, the fog and the ocean, calm at first but all too soon threatening. Creating in a single gesture the crossing of the strait and the shadow of a depression – at first kept at bay then returning with enormous force; brotherhood – love? – which, little by little, becomes unbearable, without meaning until, finally, an accident brings calm and peace and, paradoxically, lightness at last.

A journey to the heart of two entangled lives, an odyssey.

– Patrice Chéreau, Paris, March 2011

BIOGRAPHIES

The One Tom Brooke

Theatre includes: *Jerusalem* (Royal Court/West End); *The Caretaker* (Everyman, Liverpool); *Dying For It* (Almeida); *The Long and the Short and the Tall* – TMA Best Supporting Performance Award (Lyceum, Sheffield); *After the End* (Paines Plough); *Osama the Hero* (Hampstead); *Some Voices* (Young Vic).

Television includes: *Room at the Top* (Great Meadow); *Thorne: Scaredycat* (Sky); *Murder Prevention* (World Productions).

Film includes: *The Veteran* (DMK Productions); *The Boat that Rocked* (Working Title); *Venus* (Miramax).

Radio includes: *Proud*; *Like Minded People* (BBC).

The Other Jack Laskey

Theatre includes: *Sweet Nothings* (Young Vic/international tour); *As You Like It*; *A New World – A Life of Thomas Paine*; *In Extremis*; *Antony and Cleopatra* (Shakespeare's Globe); *The Tragedy of Thomas Hobbes*; *The Merchant of Venice*; *The Taming of the Shrew* (RSC); *The Masque of the Red Death* (Punchdrunk); *Hamlet* (Haymarket Theatre Basingstoke & tour); *Biloxi Blues* (Couch Potato Productions); *Hamlet* (Old Vic); *Romeo and Juliet* (Vienna's English Theatre).

TV includes: *Spilt Milk* – also co-writer (BBC); *Heartbeat* (ITV).

Film includes: *Sherlock Holmes 2* (Warner Bros.); *The Isis* (BBC Films); *A Family Portrait* (Channel 4).

Radio includes: *Arcadia* (BBC Radio 4).

Jon Fosse

Jon Fosse was born in 1959 in the Norwegian costal town of Haugesund. He grew up by the fjord in Hardanger. Since the late seventies he has lived mainly in Bergen. He has a Master's Degree in comparative literature and taught at the Academy of Writing in Bergen between 1987 and 1992 since when he has been a full-time writer.

He has written some forty books – novels, volumes of poetry, essays and works for children and, last but not least, a growing number of plays.

He has received many Norwegian literary awards and prizes – including the Hedda's Prize of Honour, the highest award of Norwegian theatre – as well as international prizes including the Austrian Nestroy Prize. Apart from Ibsen, he is the most widely performed Norwegian playwright. His books and plays have been translated into more than thirty languages.

Simon Stephens

Simon Stephen's plays include *Bluebird* (Royal Court, 1998); *Herons* (Royal Court, 2001); *Port* (Manchester Royal Exchange, 2002 – Pearson Award for Best New Play); *Country Music* (Royal Court, 2004); *On the Shore of the Wide World* (Manchester Royal Exchange / National Theatre, 2005 – Olivier Award for Best New Play); *Motortown* (Royal Court, 2006); *Harper Regan* (National Theatre, 2008); *Sea Wall* (Bush Theatre / Traverse Theatre, 2008-2009); *Pornography* (Deutsches Schauspielhaus, Hanover, 2007, Edinburgh Festival / Birmingham Rep, 2008 and Tricycle Theatre, 2009); *Punk Rock* (Lyric Hammersmith / Manchester Royal Exchange, 2009); *The Trial of Ubu* (Schauspielhaus, Essen / Toneelgroep Amsterdam, 2010); *A Thousand Stars Explode in the Sky* written in collaboration with David Eldridge and Robert Holman (Lyric Hammersmith, 2010); *Marine Parade*, a play with music written with Mark Eitzel, *Animalink* for the Brighton Festival, 2010); and *Wastwater* (Royal Court, 2011). He also writes for radio and the screen. TV includes an adaptation of *Pornography* for Coming Up (Channel 4, 2009) and *Dive* (Granada / BBC, 2009).

Direction Patrice Chéreau

Patrice Chéreau has won an outstanding international reputation in theatre, film and opera. The son of two painters, his work as an actor and director of school plays attracted widespread attention. At 16 he was hailed as a theatre prodigy. At 23 he began to direct professionally, opening a new theatre in a Paris suburb.

At 29 he staged his first opera. His celebrated production of Wagner's *Ring Cycle* for the centenary of the Bayreuth Festival (1976-1980) is regarded as a milestone and has influenced the staging of operas worldwide ever since. His most recent opera production was Janáček's *From the House of the Dead* presented at the Metropolitan Opera House in NYC, at La Scala Milan and throughout Europe. Between 1982 and 1990 he was artistic director of Théâtre des Amandiers in Nanterre, Paris where he directed most of the work of Bernard-Marie Koltès, the leading French playwright of his generation.

In the mid-1970s, Chéreau began to direct film, his first being a thriller *La chair de l'orchidée* (*Flesh of the Orchid*). Although known primarily in France for his many theatre productions, as well as as an actor, Chéreau has continued to direct award-winning, highly personal films including: *L'Homme blessé* (*The Wounded Man*, 1983), the international hit *La Reine Margot* (*Queen Margot*, 1994), *Ceux qui m'aiment prendront le train* (*Those Who Love Me Can Take the Train*, 1998), *Intimacy* (2001), *Son frère* (*His Brother*, 2003), *Gabrielle* (2005) and *Persécution* (2009).

A frequent teacher at film schools in New York and Paris, Chéreau recently took on a new role as guest curator at the Louvre where he incorporated dance, opera, theatre, film and painting in the 2010 show *Les Visages et les corps (Faces and Bodies)*. *I Am the Wind*, opening at the Young Vic, is his first-ever production in English.

Artistic Collaboration Thierry Thieû Niang

Thierry Thieû Niang works as frequently with amateurs and children as with professional artists. He has worked in a wide variety of venues, including public theatres and studios, schools, hospitals, even prisons – all to explore danced movement and its representations.

As a dancer and choreographer, his research has taken place over many years, especially in France but also in Nairobi, New York, London, Madrid, Milan and Berlin. In this work dancers, musicians, actors, visual artists and writers – often working alongside amateurs – are invited to improvise and create a language within a space where bodies and cultures can meet.

This season, Niang is working as Associate Artist with Norah Krief, Angélique Clairand, Catherine Nicolas, Lancelot Hamelin, Massed Eric and Olivier Balazuc with the Comedy of Valence at Richard Brunel. He also collaborates with Ariane Ascaride, Marie Desplechin, Clara Cornil, Julie Kretzschmar, Geoffrey Coppini, Jean Paul Wenzel, Romain Duris, Patrice Chéreau, Bastien Lefèvre and the musicians Saori Furukawa, Takumi Fukushima, Strasnoy Oscar, Klaus Janek and François Thuillier.

Set Richard Peduzzi

Richard Peduzzi, scenographer, set designer and painter, studied under sculptor Charles Auffret in Paris before embarking on a career as a painter.

Since 1967 he has designed for Patrice Chéreau, including several premieres of Bernard-Marie Koltès plays at Théâtre des Amandiers in Nanterre between 1982 and 1989 as well as *Time and the Room* by Botho Straus at Théâtre de l'Odeon.

In opera his work includes Wagner's *Ring Cycle* (1976-1980 Bayreuth conducted by Pierre Boulez), *Così Fan Tutti* (2005 Aix-en-Provence Festival), *Tristan and Isolde* (2007 La Scala, Milan) and *From the House of the Dead* by Janáček (2007 Weiner Festwochen, Aix-en-Provence festival, La Scala, Milan, Metropolitan Opera, New York). His films include *The Flesh of the Orchid* (1975), *Judith Therpauve* (1978), *The Wounded Man* (1983), *La Reine Margot* (1994) and *Those Who Love Me Can Take the Train* (1997).

Richard has been art director/curator for many museum exhibitions including *Degas, Gauguin, Titien, Impressionism – the origins* and *Chardin* for the Grand Palais, Paris, and *Mantenga, The Dream of Antiquity, Rembrandt* and *Le Lorrain* at the Louvre, as well as the opera and architecture galleries at the Musée d'Orsay (1986), the restoration, interior architecture and design for the library and museum of the Opera Garnier (1986), the presentation and interior architecture of the historical archives of the Louvre and the museum design for the Christofle silverware museum in Saint-Denis (2002).

He was director of National School of Decorative Arts (1990-2002) and director of the French Acadeny Villa Médicis in Rome (2002-2008).

Most recently, he curated Patrice Chéreau's exhibitions at the Louvre (*The Face and the Body* and *Behind the Images*, 2011).

Costumes Caroline de Vivaise

Caroline met Patrice Chéreau in the 1980s and designed the costumes for his productions of Bernard Marie Koltès' plays, from *Quay West* to his 2011 production of *The Night Just Before the Forest* with Romain Duris. She also designed the costumes for Chéreau's production of Jon Fosse's *Autumn Dream* at the Louvre and Théâtre de la Ville.

In opera, she designed costumes for Mozart's *Così Fan Tutti* and Janáček's *From the House of the Dead*.

For cinema, she worked with Chéreau on *Hôtel de France, The Wounded Man, Those Who Love Me Can Take the Train, Intimacy, His Brother, Gabrielle* (for which she won the César for Best Costume Design) and *Persecution* starring Romain Duris and Charlotte Gainsbourg. She has worked on 60 films winning a César for *Germinal* and her most recent César for *The Princess of Montpensier* directed by Bertrand Tavernier.

Light Dominique Bruguière

Dominique has worked with the Comédie Française, L'Opéra de Paris, Théâtre du Chatelet, Théâtre National de l'Odéon, Festival d'Aix-en-Provence, Festival d'Avignon, Festival de Salsbourg, Wiener Festwochen, Edinburgh Festival, Barbican, Brooklyn Academy of Music, Teatro Real in Madrid, Liceu in Barcelona, Festspielhaus in Zurich and Hambourg, Grand Théâtre de Genève, La Monnaie in Brussels and La Scala, Milan. Directors she has worked with include Dario Fo, Peter Zadek, Youssef Chahine, Deborah Warner, Robert Carsen, Jorge Lavelli, Karole Armitage, Francesca Zambello, James Ivory, Luc Bondy and Patrice Chéreau. Among recent productions are *Yvonne Princesse de Bourgogne* by Philippe Boesmans at the Théâtre Royal de la Monnaie with Luc Bondy, *Rêve d'automne* at the Louvre and Théâtre de la ville with Patrice Chéreau, *L'heure espagnole* de Maurice Ravel at l'Opéra de Paris, *Caligula* with the Opera de Paris's Ballet. For the Young Vic she lit Martin Crimp's *Cruel and Tender* directed by Luc Bondy.

She received the Prix de la Critique in 1990/2000 for her lighting of Jon Fosse's *Quelqu'un va venir,* and again in 2003/2004 for Jon Fosse's *Variations sur la mort* and *Pélléas et Mélisande*. She won a Molière (2003) for *Phèdre* directed by Patrice Chéreau.

Music Éric Neveux

On deciding to become a musician at the age of 15, Éric Neveux left his Conservatory and quit piano and music theory classes. Ten years later he met François Ozon, a young director just graduating from film school, and composed the score for his first film *Regarde La Mer* as well as the theme for his first feature *Sitcom.*

Influenced by and passionate about the emerging Bristol scene, he created his alter ego, Mr Neveux. *Tuba*, the first album under this name, was signed to Cup of Tea Records. Éric's career in film and TV soundtracks took off in 1997 when he began to work with Patrice Chéreau on his film *Those Who Love Me Can Take the Train* (Official Selection Cannes Film Festival 1997). It marked the beginning of a long collaboration spanning many projects including *Intimacy* (Golden Bear at Berlin Film Festival 2001) and *Persecution* (2009).

Through this long collaboration, Éric has played with genre, texture, and ambiance. From comedy to drama, full orchestra to electro-acoustic, independent to mass-audience. He approaches each project as a blank page, a new effort to collaborate fully with the director's vision.

Casting Sam Jones CDG

Sam was until recently Head of Casting for the RSC. She has just cast the opening year for the newly formed National Theatre Wales.

Her extensive theatre credits include: work for Peter Hall, Stephen Berkoff, Kneehigh, Shared Experience, Told By An Idiot, The Opera Group, Sheffield Crucible, West Yorkshire Playhouse, Hampstead Theatre, the Almeida and the Royal Court.

Her work for the West End includes: *Another Country, Journey's End, Dinner, A Day in the Death of Joe Egg, Up for Grabs!*, *After Mrs Rochester* and *The Children's Hour.*

Her work for the Young Vic includes: *Cruel and Tender, Sweet Nothings, Amazonia, Festa!* and *Electra.*

Her recent television work includes: several series of *Trial and Retribution, The Commander* and *Above Suspicion* for La Plante/ITV, and the BAFTA award-winning *Occupation* and *Lennon Naked* for the BBC.

Recent film work includes: *Resistance.*

Assistant Direction Peter Cant

Assistant direction: *Sweet Nothings*; *Joe Turner's Come and Gone*; *Private Lives* (Hampstead).

As writer and director: *Opera 3* (Snape Maltings, Aldeburgh Music); *We Feel Fine* (Arcola Studio K); *Little Thorns* (The Capital Centre); *The Elephant Tree* (Edinburgh Fringe); *Living on the Borderline* (Caracol YCD, Belize).

As director: *Hearts and Minds* (Theatre 503).

As writer: *we feel fine* (Theatre 503, Tristan Bates); *London Wall* (Soho Theatre); *The Pleiades* (Greenwich Royal Observatory).

The Young Vic

'The Young Vic is one of our favourite theatres, resolutely going its own way as bustling and unorthodox as ever.'
The Sunday Times

'The vibrant Waterloo powerhouse'
Time Out

Our shows
We present the widest variety of classics, new plays, forgotten works and music theatre. We tour and co-produce extensively within the UK and internationally.

Our artists
Our shows are created by some of the world's great theatre people alongside the most adventurous of the younger generation.
This fusion makes the Young Vic one of the most exciting theatres in the world.

Our audience
... is famously the youngest and most diverse in London. We encourage those who don't think theatre is 'for them' to make it part of their lives. We give 10% of our tickets to schools and neighbours irrespective of box office demand, and keep prices low.

Our partners near at hand
Each year we engage with 10,000 local people – individuals and groups of all kinds including schools and colleges – by exploring theatre on and off stage. From time to time we invite our neighbours to appear on our stage alongside professionals.

Our partners further away
By co-producing with leading theatre, opera, and dance companies from around the world we challenge ourselves and create shows neither partner could achieve alone.

The Young Vic is a company limited by guarantee, registered in England No. 1188209
VAT Registration No. 236 673 348

The Young Vic (registered charity no. 268876) receives public funding from:

Supported by
ARTS COUNCIL ENGLAND

The Young Vic Company

Supporting the Young Vic

The Young Vic relies on the generous support of many trusts, companies and individuals to continue our work, on and off stage. For their recent support we thank

Public Funders
Arts Council England
Lambeth Borough Council
London Development Agency
Southwark Council

Corporate Supporters
American Airlines
Barclays Capital
Bloomberg
HSBC Bank plc
KPMG Foundation
Markit

The Directors' Circle

Big Cheeses
Bloomberg
Cantor Fitzgerald
HgCapital
Ingenious Media Plc
Land Securities
Sense Worldwide

Hot Shots
Clifford Chance
Lane Consulting
Slaughter and May
Taylor Wessing LLP

Trust Supporters
29th May 1961
    Charitable Trust
The City Bridge Trust
Fund of the Capital
    Community Foundation
    Dorset Foundation
Clore Duffield Foundation
D'Oyly Carte Charitable Trust
The Drapers' Company
Equitable Charitable Trust
Eranda Foundation
Esmée Fairbairn Foundation
Foundation for Sport
    & the Arts
French Embassy in the UK
Garfield Weston Foundation
Genesis Foundation

Goethe-Institut
Goldsmiths' Company
Gosling Foundation
Harold Hyam Wingate
    Foundation
Henry Smith Charity
Institut français
    du Royaume-Uni
Jerwood Charitable
    Foundation
John Ellerman Foundation
John Thaw Foundation
The Limbourne Trust
Linbury Trust
Man Group plc Charitable
    Trust
Martin Bowley Charitable
    Trust
Medicor Foundation
Peter Minet Trust
The Progress Foundation
The Royal Victoria Hall
    Foundation
Trust for London
The Worshipful Company of
    Grocers

Production Partnership
Tony & Gisela Bloom
Kay Ellen Consolver &
    John Storkerson
Chris & Jane Lucas
Miles Morland
Nadine Majaro &
    Roger Pilgrim

Best Friends
Jane Attias
Chris & Frances Bates
Anthony & Karen Beare
Royce & Rotha Bell
The Bickertons
Katie Bradford
Jennifer & Jeff Eldredge
Sarah Hall
Richard Hardman & Family
Susan & Richard Hayden
Nik Holttum & Helen Brannigan

Suzanne & Michael Johnson
Tom Keatinge
John Kinder & Gerry Downey
Carol Lake
Anna Lane
Simon & Midge Palley
Naomi Russell
Charles & Donna Scott
Justin Shinebourne
The Tracy Family
Leo & Susan van der Linden
Edgar & Judith Wallner
Rob Wallace
Andrew Wylde

Great Friends
Angus Aynsley &
    Miel de Botton Aynsley
Tim & Caroline Clark
Robyn Durie
Susan Hyland
Stephen & Angela Jordan
Ann Lewis
Tony Mackintosh
Ian McKellen
Barbara Minto
Georgia Oetker
Anthony & Sally Salz
Jon & Noralee Sedmak
Bhagat Sharma
Mr & Mrs Bruce R. Snider
Jan & Michael Topham
The Ulrich Family
Donna & Richard Vinter
Jimmy & Carol Walker

Théâtre de la Ville

DIRECTION EMMANUEL DEMARCY-MOTA

PARIS

Rhinocéros // E. Ionesco // E. Demarcy-Mota
29 april - 14 may © J.-L. FERNANDEZ

Théâtre de la Ville is dedicated to international creation based on the coalition of different art forms: theatre, dance and music.

Developing a programme open to the word and its artistic experiments, it invites great international masters in all disciplines, while paying particular attention to the revelation of upcoming young artists. In recent years, it has developed innovative partnerships with leading theatres in Europe and the world.

Presenting 90 different programmes and close to 400 performances yearly, it attracts an audience of 250,000 spectators. Théâtre de la Ville is highly involved with the City of Paris and its population, working for the development, diversity and renewal of its audience.

Pina Bausch // Tanztheater Wuppertal
last creation 22 june - 8 july © L. PHILIPPE

At Théâtre de la Ville, the richness and diversity of art forms fosters new and original ways of reaching a better image and comprehension of life and the world.

I am the wind

by **JON FOSSE**
english language version by **SIMON STEPHENS**
directed by **PATRICE CHÉREAU**
artistic collaboration **THIERRY THIEÛ NIANG**
→ in Théâtre de la Ville-Paris
from 3 to 12 june
A partnership between the Young Vic & Théâtre de la Ville-Paris

4 indian concerts from april to june © SENSE WORLD MUSIC

MAIRIE DE PARIS

I AM THE WIND

Jon Fosse

I AM THE WIND

English Language Version
by Simon Stephens

OBERON BOOKS
LONDON

WWW.OBERONBOOKS.COM

First published in 2011 by Oberon Books Ltd
521 Caledonian Road, London N7 9RH
Tel: +44 (0) 20 7607 3637 / Fax: +44 (0) 20 7607 3629
e-mail: info@oberonbooks.com
www.oberonbooks.com

A catalogue record for this book is available from the British
Library.

ISBN: 978-1-84943-071-5

Cover photography by Simon Annand.

The boat and the actions that surround it should be evoked or suggested rather than represented mimetically.

Characters

THE ONE

THE OTHER

THE ONE

I didn't want to

I just did it

THE OTHER

You just did it

THE ONE

I just did it

Short pause

THE OTHER

It just happened

But you were

so afraid it would happen

Short pause

You said that to me

quite short pause

You told me about it

THE ONE

I know

Pause

THE OTHER

And then it happened

Quite short pause

Exactly that which you were afraid would happen

Quite short pause

Exactly that which you were afraid you would do

quite short pause

it happened

Short pause

THE ONE

It did

Pause

THE OTHER

It's awful

THE ONE

I'm fine

THE OTHER

Really

THE ONE

I've gone now

I left with the wind

THE OTHER

You left

THE ONE

I've gone

Short pause

I'm not here any more

breaks off

THE OTHER

You're not here

THE ONE

No I'm not here

Short pause

THE OTHER

But

THE ONE

What

THE OTHER

Okay

short pause

right

short pause

but life

quite short pause

it's not too bad

is it

quite short pause

there are so many places

you could be

THE ONE

> *short pause*
> Yeah there are
> or maybe there's
> nowhere
> *quite short pause*
> but then you have to
> well
> *quite short pause*
> people have to be somewhere
> *short pause*
> I can't bear the noise
> *quite short pause*
> I can't bear the noise other people make
> I can't bear the noise of everything
> *quite short pause*
> it weighs me down
> it overwhelms me
> *Quite short pause*

THE OTHER

> You want to be on your own

THE ONE

> I can't be on my own

THE OTHER

> You can't be on your own
> you can't be with anybody else

THE ONE

> I can't bear all the noise

THE OTHER

> You need quiet

THE ONE

> I need quiet
> *quite short pause*
> and I want
> everything to be less visible

THE OTHER
>Visible

THE ONE
>Everything's so visible
>everything can be seen
>the things that people hide with what they say
>the things maybe they don't even know about themselves
>I see all of that

THE OTHER
>You don't want to be around other people

THE ONE
>No

THE OTHER
>But you don't want to be on your own
>Why don't you want to be on your own

THE ONE
>Because if I'm on my own
>then all I can see is myself
>and all I can hear is myself
>*quite short pause*
>And I don't like that
>*quite short pause*
>obviously
>*quite short pause*
>I mean
>*breaks off*

THE OTHER
>Isn't it better though

THE ONE
>No it's not better
>*quite short pause*
>of course it's not better
>*quite short pause*
>it's worse

THE OTHER

Don't you like yourself

THE ONE

No

THE OTHER

You don't like other people

and you don't like yourself

THE ONE

Yes

short pause

that's about the size of it

Pause

THE OTHER

What is it you don't like

about yourself

THE ONE

I don't like that I'm worthless

THE OTHER

You're worthless

THE ONE

Yes

Pause

THE OTHER

How can you say that

Of course you're not worthless

You're worth so much

THE ONE

Alright I'm not worthless

short pause

but if I'm on my own

quite short pause

and all I can hear is myself

right

then

breaks off

THE OTHER

     Then what

THE ONE

     Then there's nothing there

     quite short pause

     and then I start getting heavy

THE OTHER

     You start getting heavy

THE ONE

     Yes

THE OTHER

     Heavy

THE ONE

     I turn into a rock

     quite short pause

     and it gets

     the rock

     gets heavier and heavier

     quite short pause

     I get so heavy

     that I can barely move

     quite short pause

     so heavy that I

     that I sink

     quite short pause

     down and down

     quite short pause

     down under the sea

     I sink

     down to the bottom

     and then

     quite short pause

     I just lie there

     at the bottom of the sea

       Heavy

       Motionless

THE OTHER

       And then

       right when you're a rock

       quite short pause

       then

       then you don't say anything

THE ONE

       I can barely speak

       quite short pause

       it's a struggle

       to get a single word out

       to extract a single word

       quite short pause

       and then

       when the word is out

       when the word has been spoken

       it feels so heavy

       quite short pause

       that it drags me down too

       quite short pause

       it makes me sink and sink

THE OTHER

       Is that what it's like

       The words get heavy

THE ONE

       Yes

       Short pause

THE OTHER

       But why is it like that

THE ONE

       It's just the way it is

       Short pause

THE OTHER

You're a rock

Quite short pause

And you're grey

quite short pause

like a rock

THE ONE

Yes

quite short pause

like

breaks off

No not exactly

THE OTHER

What

not exactly

THE ONE

Not grey

THE OTHER

What do you mean

THE ONE

You said grey

It's not grey

THE OTHER

No

THE ONE

No because it's nice

grey

THE OTHER

Nice

THE ONE

Yes nice

and ugly

quite short pause

grey is the bare little islands and reefs

look out there

look over there

You see the little islands and the reefs

They're all grey

THE OTHER

It's nice

quite short pause

and ugly

THE ONE

Yes

THE OTHER

Like the fog

THE ONE

yeah like the fog you see out

in the ocean

a bit like the fog

quite short pause

perhaps

Quite short pause

No it's not grey

like the fog

quite short pause

more like

THE OTHER

What

THE ONE

continues

more like

okay

yeah maybe

yes maybe more like a concrete wall

THE OTHER

It's like everything is just a concrete wall

THE ONE

> I'm a concrete wall
> that's breaking into pieces

THE OTHER

> That must hurt

THE ONE

> Of course it hurts

THE OTHER

> Does it just hurt

THE ONE

> Yes

THE OTHER

> All you are
> *quite short pause*
> is a concrete wall
> that's breaking into pieces

THE ONE

> And falling apart
> *quite short pause*
> falling into rubble

THE OTHER

> You're rubble

THE ONE

> No I'm the breaking
> no not that either

THE OTHER

> The cracking

THE ONE

> Yeah in a way
> *quite short pause*
> maybe
> *quite short pause*
> maybe I'm the cracking

THE OTHER

> You're the cracking

THE ONE

Yes

quite short pause

or

quite short pause

all this is just words

just something you say

THE OTHER

You're a concrete wall

That's cracking to pieces

THE ONE

It's just words

Pause

THE OTHER

But

quite short pause

okay will you tell me

quite short pause

what makes it better

why you like

to go

quite short pause

out on the water

THE ONE

Well I could

Short pause

THE OTHER

Well do

THE ONE

I

pause

I

right

short pause

can you see over there
the little islands and the reefs
over there
points
those cliffs
the grey ones
the pure grey cliffs
quite short pause
and can you see the rocks on the beach
big
round
grey
can you see them
quite short pause
there
over there

THE OTHER

Yes

THE ONE

And can you see that cove
quite short pause
there
where the little island sort of spreads its legs
quite short pause
where it makes a cove
points
over there
can you see that

THE OTHER

Yes

THE ONE

We could anchor there
The boat would be safe there
Quite short pause
Do you want to

Quite short pause

Do you want to go there

THE OTHER

Okay

short pause

we could do

THE ONE

Come on then

THE ONE pushes the tiller and the boat glides slowly towards the cove.

THE OTHER

It looks quite nice there

Quite short pause

And the sea looks calm

Quite short pause

All the islands and the reefs

And the ocean

quite short pause

out there

quite short pause

is that the open ocean

THE ONE

Yes

THE OTHER

And then

right in front of us

between us and the ocean

on this side of that little island

is a nice sheltered cove

THE ONE

And we can cast anchor there and

quite short pause

if we want to

we could stay there till tomorrow

THE OTHER

    Is it safe there

THE ONE

    The weather's perfect

THE OTHER

    The wind won't pick up

    I mean there's a bit of fog

    Isn't there out there on the ocean

THE ONE

    No

    quite short pause

    no I don't think so

THE OTHER

    Are you sure

THE ONE

    Well you can never be quite sure

    Pause

    Let's sail there

THE OTHER

    Okay let's

THE ONE

    You want to

THE OTHER

    Why not

THE ONE

    Great

    Pause

THE OTHER

    You like everything to be silent don't you

THE ONE

    Yes

    Quite short pause

THE OTHER
>Is that why
>you like
>being at sea so much

THE ONE
>Maybe

THE OTHER
>Do you like being at sea so much
>because you want everything to be silent

THE ONE
>I don't know if I do want it to be silent
>And there are noises on the water too
>Creaking
>Fluttering
>Screeching
>*Short pause*

THE OTHER
>But you don't like noise

THE ONE
>No
>*quite short pause*
>or
>*breaks off*

THE OTHER
>And it's quiet on the water
>*quite short pause*
>the sounds are really quite quiet there

THE ONE
>Yes
>*quite short pause*
>in a way
>it is quiet out there

THE OTHER

But when life lives things can be heard

things can be seen

That's just how it is

THE ONE

That's right

Pause

THE OTHER

And you don't like that

Pause

You don't like that life lives

Pause

Because if you had liked that

breaks off. Pause

But you like being on the water

THE ONE

Yes

Pause

No

quite short pause

no

quite short pause

no I

breaks off

THE OTHER

What

THE ONE

Well

quite short pause

I'm here

I have my place

everyone has their place

I have my place

Everything has its place

Short pause

THE OTHER

      But you shouldn't be here

      quite short pause

      should you

      not here in the boat

      I mean

      breaks off

THE ONE

      I am here

THE OTHER

      But you don't want to be here

THE ONE

      I don't want to be anywhere else either

THE OTHER

      You don't want anything

      short pause

      is it possible not to want anything

      quite short pause

      when you're cold

      you want to put some clothes on

      quite short pause

      don't you

      or warm up

      somehow

THE ONE

      Yes

      Pause

THE OTHER

      And when you're hungry

      or thirsty

      right

      breaks off

THE ONE

      Then you want something to eat

      or something to drink

THE OTHER

> That's right
> *Short pause*
> And don't you want those things

THE ONE

> Now and then
> *Pause*

THE OTHER

> Then you do want something

THE ONE

> Maybe
> *quite short pause*
> if that's what it means to want

THE OTHER

> Isn't it

THE ONE

> Maybe it's only because we're here that
> *breaks off, quite short pause*
> that all those things
> *breaks off, quite short pause*
> yes all those things you're talking about
> *breaks off, short pause*

THE OTHER

> Maybe
> *Pause*
> But if someone
> Me
> right if I hit you

THE ONE

> Then I'd try to defend myself

THE OTHER

> Isn't that about wanting

THE ONE

> It might be
> *Quite short pause*

Or it might just be because it really hurts getting hit
Pause

THE OTHER

But life must live

THE ONE

Life must live

THE OTHER

And you
quite short pause
you don't like that

THE ONE

No I do

THE OTHER

How can you
quite short pause
how
OK I
breaks off

THE ONE

Because it isn't always like that

THE OTHER

It's not always like you've said

THE ONE

No
short pause
no it can be different sometimes
every now and then it isn't like that

THE OTHER

It's different
at sea

THE ONE

Yes
Pause

THE OTHER

>And when you were a child
>
>was it like that then

THE ONE

>No

THE OTHER

>What was it like then

THE ONE

>Then everything was in motion
>
>*Pause. THE ONE goes and lifts up the anchor*
>
>But now
>
>*quite short pause*
>
>we're here
>
>look
>
>we're in our cove

THE OTHER

>Right
>
>*THE ONE drops the anchor*

THE ONE

>But
>
>*quite short pause*
>
>right why don't you go out on the deck
>
>*quite short pause*
>
>go to the bow
>
>and get ready to moor the boat
>
>*quite short pause*
>
>the rope
>
>lives up in the bow
>
>*points*
>
>yes there
>
>there in that crate
>
>*points*
>
>but hurry up

                 points

                 right

                 now go now

THE OTHER

                 And then what

THE ONE

                 quite short pause

                 Then

                 when we reach the shore

                 right

                 then you jump off

THE OTHER

                 And then what

THE ONE

                 Then you moor the boat

THE OTHER

                 Right

THE ONE

                 Well go on then

                 We've not got all day

                 Hurry up

THE OTHER

                 Right

                 quite short pause

                 I am hurrying actually

                 Can't you tell

                 THE OTHER goes out on the deck and walks forward, finds a rope

THE ONE

                 Now

                 jump now

                 Quite short pause

                 Go on jump

                 Jump ashore

                 THE OTHER jumps, slips, falls, hurts himself

                 Did you hurt yourself

THE OTHER

    I slipped

    THE OTHER tries to stand up, gets to his feet, but is in pain

THE ONE

    Are you alright

THE OTHER

    Yes

    quite short pause

    I think so

    I just bashed myself a little

THE ONE

    Right

THE OTHER

    But I'm alright

THE ONE

    Now tie the rope there

    quite short pause

    yes there

    quite short pause

    to that bolt you see over there

THE OTHER

    I'll try

    Pause

THE ONE

    Is it sore

THE OTHER

    A bit

    yeah

    short pause

THE ONE

    Right

    But hurry up will you

    please

THE OTHER

    Okay

short pause

now what do you want me to do

THE ONE

You've got to tie the rope to that

quite short pause

to that bolt you see over there

THE OTHER

And then what

THE ONE

And then you get back into the boat

THE OTHER

I can't get back

The boat's too far away

THE ONE

Just pull it towards you

THE OTHER

Okay

Quite short pause

THE OTHER pulls the boat a little further in

I can't get it any closer

THE ONE

No

Short pause

Can you get back on board

THE OTHER

I'll have a go

THE OTHER jumps and grabs the rail and crawls back on deck

THE ONE

That didn't look easy

THE OTHER

No

quite short pause

no

but I did it

THE ONE

      Yup

      Pause

THE OTHER

      And now ok right

      quite short pause

      now that the boat's moored

      breaks off, quite short pause

      what happens now

      Pause

THE ONE

      Well

      Short pause

      When you've cast anchor

      then

      quite short pause

      then

      quite short pause

      then you have yourself a drink

THE OTHER

      A wee dram

THE ONE

      It's just what you do

      short pause

      shall I pour us one

THE OTHER

      Yeah

      A drink would be terrific

      THE ONE goes to fetch a bottle and glasses

THE ONE

      I think it's exactly what we need

      THE ONE gives both glasses to THE OTHER, pours, takes one glass

      That'll hit the spot

      Short pause. THE ONE puts the bottle down

      Cheers

THE OTHER

> Cheers
>
> *They raise their glasses and drink*

THE ONE

> Oh that's lovely
>
> *Pause*
>
> Great here
>
> isn't it
>
> *quite short pause*
>
> the grey reefs
>
> all bare
>
> nothing grows here
>
> *quite short pause*
>
> the bare little islands
>
> all grey and black
>
> and the rocks on the seashore
>
> the round rocks
>
> *quite short pause*
>
> and then
>
> out there
>
> *short pause*
>
> behind there
>
> there's the ocean
>
> *quite short pause*
>
> and there
>
> is where the ocean and sky meet
>
> *quite short pause*
>
> the ocean's so calm

THE OTHER

> Yeah

THE ONE

> Nothing grows here
>
> *quite short pause*
>
> it's all grey rock

THE OTHER

    And there are so many little islands here

    so many reefs

    Quite short pause

    And the ocean

    And the sky

    Long pause. THE ONE fills their glasses, they drink

THE ONE

    I do like a drink

THE OTHER

    Yeah

    Short pause

THE ONE

    And it's so quiet here

THE OTHER

    All you can hear

    is the sea lapping against the boat

THE ONE

    Yes

    and we just float

    nice and light

    quite short pause

    we're so light

    it's sort of like

    quite short pause

    there's wind in us

THE OTHER

    It's like we're rolling

THE ONE

    Yes

    Yes that's good

THE OTHER

    And the boat's rolling

THE ONE

Rolling lightly

Rolling gently

quite short pause

that's exactly the way it is

THE OTHER

We're so light

We're as light as the wind

quite short pause

nearly

THE ONE

And we're rolling too

high up here

quite short pause

lightly

with the boat

THE OTHER

Yes

Pause

Yes

quite short pause

we're so light

quite short pause

yes

quite short pause

but you

quite short pause

a while ago

you said

that every now and then

you were so heavy

quite short pause

that you were a rock

THE ONE

Yeah

Short pause

THE OTHER

What did you mean by that

THE ONE

Nothing

THE OTHER

You must've meant something

THE ONE

They were just words

It was just something I said

I didn't mean anything

THE OTHER

Just something you said

THE ONE

Yes

quite short pause

yes just words

THE OTHER

Rock

The word rock

THE ONE

It's just something you say

THE OTHER

Right

THE ONE

Yup

quite short pause

it's not real

quite short pause

you try to say how something is

by saying something else

THE OTHER

Because you can't say

how it really is

THE ONE

No

quite short pause

no of course you can't

Short pause

THE OTHER

It just becomes words

THE ONE

Words words and more words

Pause

THE OTHER

But what you said

quite short pause

right that thing about being a concrete wall

which is cracking

THE ONE

That was badly put

THE OTHER

It was an image

THE ONE

Yes

quite short pause

yes I suppose you could

call it an image

THE OTHER

And an image

breaks off

THE ONE

Yes I suppose it says something

quite short pause

something small

quite short pause

53

but mostly it says something wrong

quite short pause

something that's not supposed to be said

THE OTHER

An image

should say how something is

quite short pause

because you just can't say it any other way

That's the whole point of it I suppose

THE ONE

Yes

I think so

THE OTHER

But in the end it always says something else

THE ONE

That's what I think

quite short pause

I think maybe all words are like that

quite short pause

but the essence of something

how it really is

you can't communicate that

because right

that's not a word is it

THE OTHER

It's something that is there

Quite short pause

And something that isn't

breaks off

THE ONE

Yes

Short pause

But

short pause

all those things I say

I know

People shouldn't say things like that

Short pause

I know

There's no point in saying anything really

But

quite short pause

but I

quite short pause

I'm alive

so I've got to say something

quite short pause

And now

breaks off

THE OTHER

Yes what now

Quite short pause

What happens now

THE ONE

Does something have to happen

THE OTHER

Well we can't just stay here

quite short pause

in the boat

quite short pause

THE ONE

Course we can

THE OTHER

Well we could

THE ONE

It's so quiet now

THE OTHER

Yeah

quite short pause

yes now everything alive

is quiet

Short pause

THE ONE

Don't you love it

THE OTHER

Yes I do

THE ONE

Not really

THE OTHER

Well no I do

quite short pause

but I don't think I understand it completely

quite short pause

I don't think I completely understand

what's so good about it

THE ONE

No

THE OTHER

Can you tell me

THE ONE

No

quite short pause

no it's the same

THE OTHER

As before

THE ONE

Yes

Pause

Yes I really like it

I just like

everything when it's so quiet

quite short pause

and the light wind

I like that too

quite short pause

I like
quite short pause
being light
rocking gently
in the heavy boat
quite short pause
It's good

THE OTHER

Yeah

THE ONE

I just like being in the boat

THE OTHER

Yes
quite short pause
I think I
breaks off
yes me too
I like the smell of the sea as well
Short pause
And I like looking
at the rocks on the seashore
quite short pause
or the reefs
or the little islands
Quite short pause
I like looking at
the sky
And at the ocean
And I like
quite short pause
just being in the boat
I didn't think that I
would like that
But I do

THE ONE

> Yeah
>
> *Pause*
>
> I like
>
> that out there
>
> *quite short pause, points*
>
> is the sea
>
> cold and dangerous
>
> calm and vast
>
> *quite short pause*
>
> and if you lie there
>
> *short pause*
>
> in the sea
>
> it wouldn't take long
>
> *breaks off*

THE OTHER

> You'd freeze to death really quickly
>
> You'd be dead
>
> *quite short pause*
>
> be gone forever

THE ONE

> That's right
>
> *Pause*
>
> We're completely attached to
>
> *breaks off, short pause*
>
> without the boat
>
> *short pause*
>
> a couple of steps to the right
>
> *short pause*
>
> and we're finished

THE OTHER

> *Short pause*
>
> But do you quite like
>
> *quite short pause*
>
> do you quite like thinking about that

THE ONE

> Yes
>
> *quite short pause*
>
> I do

THE OTHER

> Isn't it frightening

THE ONE

> Yeah
>
> Yes of course it is

THE OTHER

> Because
>
> *quite short pause*
>
> this boat's really small
>
> *breaks off*

THE ONE

> Yeah

THE OTHER

> And on the sea
>
> on the ocean
>
> this big wide ocean
>
> you might have to be there
>
> on the boat
>
> for days
>
> for weeks

THE ONE

> Yeah
>
> *Short pause*

THE OTHER

> And you'd like that

THE ONE

> Yes

THE OTHER

> Always

THE ONE

> No not always
>
> *Pause*

THE OTHER

When don't you like it

THE ONE

When I'm on my own

THE OTHER

You don't like being on your own in the boat

THE ONE

No

THE OTHER

Why not

THE ONE

No

short pause

it's nothing

THE OTHER

Say it

THE ONE

No

THE OTHER

Do you get frightened

THE ONE

Yes

no

quite short pause

no not frightened exactly

but

breaks off

THE OTHER

What are you frightened of

THE ONE

Of

breaks off

THE OTHER

Say it

THE ONE
>	I get frightened that I'll jump

THE OTHER
>	Jump into the sea

THE ONE
>	Yes
>	*Pause*

THE OTHER
>	Do you think about that a lot

THE ONE
>	All the time

THE OTHER
>	You think about it all the time
>	when you're on your own in the boat

THE ONE
>	Yes
>	*quite short pause*
>	well not exactly think
>	but
>	*breaks off*

THE OTHER
>	You're on your own a lot
>	in the boat

THE ONE
>	Yes

THE OTHER
>	And it's always there

THE ONE
>	Always
>	*Short pause*

THE OTHER
>	As a thought

THE ONE
>	Not exactly as a thought
>	*quite short pause*

or maybe as a thought

quite short pause

but

short pause

yes as a thought as well

quite short pause

but

I think mostly as a fear

quite short pause

no that's wrong

THE OTHER

That's just words

THE ONE

Yes

THE OTHER

But it's something that's close

It's there

quite short pause

not quite as a thought

not quite as a fear

but as something close

THE ONE

Yes

quite short pause

yeah maybe

THE OTHER

Do you ever forget it

THE ONE

Yes

quite short pause

that happens

quite short pause

no

Pause

THE OTHER

    It's close to you all the time

THE ONE

    Pretty much

THE OTHER

    But you don't think about it

    when you're not alone

    in the boat

THE ONE

    No

    quite short pause

    no then

    then it goes

    Pause

THE OTHER

    There's

    breaks off

THE ONE

    There's not much I can say about it

    THE ONE wants to refill THE OTHER's glass, but he holds up his hand

THE OTHER

    No thanks

    not for me

    THE ONE fills his own glass

    It was nice

    but

    breaks off

THE ONE

    Yeah

THE OTHER

    It calms you down

    a drink does calm you down

THE ONE

It does

Pause

THE OTHER

So

quite short pause

so here we are

in the boat

short pause

and

short pause

THE ONE

Shall I get us something to eat

Just something simple

THE OTHER

That'd be nice

that

THE ONE

Or we can set sail

THE OTHER

And then what

THE ONE

Then we sail

THE OTHER

And then what

THE ONE

And then we could find ourselves another cove

where we could cast anchor

THE OTHER

pause

Is that all

THE ONE

Yes

Short pause

I think so

Pause

THE OTHER

Perhaps we could head off for a bit

THE ONE

Course we could

THE OTHER

I wonder if it is safe here

I'm just thinking about tonight

The wind could pick up

And the ocean

quite short pause

the ocean's just there

The fog's settled out there

It's foggy out on the ocean

And out there

between us and the open sea

all there is is that little island

the grey rock

THE ONE

I know

Quite short pause

But I don't think the wind will pick up

Quite short pause

The ocean's still

The sky's clear

THE OTHER

It might not

Quite short pause

THE ONE

I'll get us something to eat

THE OTHER

That'd be nice

*THE ONE goes and lights the stove, places a pan on it, opens
a tin and pours the content in the pot*

I am

I am a bit hungry actually

THE ONE

Food always tastes better at sea

THE OTHER

I could do with something to eat

THE ONE

Yeah

Long pause

But you

THE OTHER

What

THE ONE

Food always tastes better at sea

Okay

but I thought

breaks off, quite short pause. THE ONE stirs the pot

THE OTHER

What

THE ONE

No nothing

Quite short pause

I'll lay the table

Short pause. THE ONE fetches plates and cutlery, lays the table

THE OTHER

Would you like a glass of wine with your food

Have you got any wine

THE ONE

Yes

yes I have

Short pause

I'll open a bottle of wine

THE ONE goes to get a bottle of wine, opens it, pours one glass
for THE OTHER and one for himself

THE OTHER

    I'm really hungry now

    It must be true

    that you get hungry

    being out at sea

THE ONE

    Yes

THE OTHER

    It must be the sea air

    quite short pause

    well it must be something

THE ONE

    It must be

    THE ONE lifts his glass

    Cheers

    THE OTHER lifts his glass

THE OTHER

    Cheers

    They drink. Pause

THE OTHER

    But well

    quite short pause

    life

    right it's not all that bad

    It's not always

    breaks off

THE ONE

    No

THE OTHER

    Sometimes its good

    to be alive

THE ONE

> Yes

THE OTHER

> It's only every so often that you
>
> well
>
> how did you put it
>
> that you're a rock
>
> or something

THE ONE

> Yes
>
> *quite short pause*
>
> yes a lot of the time I'm not

THE OTHER

> No
>
> *Pause*

THE ONE

> But
>
> *quite short pause*
>
> do you know
>
> I think the food might be ready
>
> It just needed warming up
>
> It's quite a simple meal
>
> You know

THE OTHER

> I know that

THE ONE

> Simple but good
>
> I hope
>
> *THE ONE puts his glass down, goes and fetches the pot*
>
> It's food anyway
>
> And I hope
>
> you'll enjoy it
>
> *THE ONE serves THE OTHER*
>
> Here you go

THE OTHER

    Thank you

    THE ONE serves food to himself and puts the pot away and
    THE OTHER starts to eat

    Mmm

    Lovely

    This is delicious

THE ONE

    Yeah I can't wait for mine

    THE ONE starts to eat. Pause

THE OTHER

    Yeah

    Short pause

    Life's not all that bad

    is it

    quite short pause

    there's good food

    quite short pause

    this is really good

    good simple food

    it's lovely

    quite short pause

    and the wine

    there's good wine

    too

    quite short pause

    and it's good to talk to people

    quite short pause

    to be together

    quite short pause

    and even if

    right

    yeah even if you have those thoughts

    quite short pause

    you know that thing about jumping

you still like being in the boat
don't you

THE ONE

Well

quite short pause

yes that's true

quite short pause

it's just every so often

that I

breaks off

THE OTHER

That you kind of

quite short pause

can't move

quite short pause

that you're a rock

sort of

THE ONE

Yes

Short pause

THE OTHER

And then

short pause

it helps

to have a drink

a wee dram

quite short pause

a glass of wine

doesn't it

THE ONE

Yes

THE OTHER

And to imagine things

short pause

what I mean
what I'm trying to say is
quite short pause
that that helps
too

THE ONE

And in a way
even being on the water
is something you imagine
kind of
quite short pause
isn't it I mean
even if you are there

THE OTHER

For sure
Short pause
Everything is
imagined
somehow
created
somehow
made up
isn't it
quite short pause
even if it actually happens
it's still imagined
quite short pause
it exists somewhere else too
in a way
quite short pause
it happens anyway
doesn't it
in words
or

breaks off, short pause

I mean

breaks off

THE ONE

Yeah

Long pause

THE OTHER

The food was lovely

THE OTHER lifts his glass

Cheers

then

THE ONE lifts his glass

THE ONE

Yeah cheers

They clink glasses

But

THE OTHER

What

THE ONE

But right

short pause

I don't know you

THE OTHER

No

quite short pause

maybe not

maybe not all that well

quite short pause

but you know me

quite short pause

you know me a bit

at least

Pause

THE ONE

    I want to say something to you

    quite short pause

    but I don't know what it is

THE OTHER

    Right

THE ONE

    I want to tell you something

THE OTHER

    short pause

    But you can't get it out

THE ONE

    No

    quite short pause

    I only know

    that I want to say something

    tell you something

    quite short pause

    because to live

    breaks off

THE OTHER

    To live

THE ONE

    Yes to live

    quite short pause

    it's

    I mean

    You have to

    breaks off

THE OTHER

    What

THE ONE

    No it's nothing

    Pause

THE OTHER

>And now
>
>*quite short pause*
>
>now that we've eaten
>
>yes
>
>*quite short pause*
>
>yes what do we do now

THE ONE

>Now we can head on our way

THE OTHER

>Right
>
>*Pause*
>
>I'll clear the table

THE ONE

>I can do it

THE OTHER

>No I'll do it
>
>And then I'll do the dishes

THE ONE

>The dishes can wait

THE OTHER

>And you can have a drink

THE ONE

>Will you have one with me

THE OTHER

>No thanks
>
>*THE ONE pours himself a drink and THE OTHER clears the table, puts the dishes in the sink*
>
>And then we'll head on our way
>
>*Quite short pause*
>
>That'll be nice
>
>I think maybe I'm starting to like it here
>
>out on the water
>
>*Pause*
>
>But

quite short pause

right

pause

is there anything else you like to think about

THE ONE

I don't have to think about anything any more

THE OTHER

Don't you

THE ONE

No

THE OTHER

You're feeling better now

THE ONE

Yes

Pause

THE OTHER

That's good

Pause

THE ONE

So now

quite short pause

now

quite short pause

we'll set sail

quite short pause

and first

quite short pause

first we've got to do what we did when we dropped
anchor

you've got to go out on the deck

and pull the boat towards the shore

THE OTHER

Okay

THE ONE

And then you've got to jump ashore and
quite short pause
untie the rope
pull the boat to the shore again
jump on board
coil up the rope
and put it in the crate
on the deck

THE OTHER

Right
*THE OTHER goes out on the deck, pulls the boat
towards the shore, jumps out, slips, lays on the rock*
Fuck
It's bloody slippery here
*THE OTHER gets to his feet and unties the rope, pulls the
boat in*
How can I get back on board
It's completely impossible

THE ONE

You've got to try
You've just got to jump
Just try

THE OTHER

I can't

THE ONE

Try to pull the boat a bit closer in

THE OTHER

Right

THE ONE

Does that work

THE OTHER

A bit
I've got it a bit closer

THE ONE

    Can you get hold of the gunwale

THE OTHER

    No

THE ONE

    You can't

THE OTHER

    No

THE ONE

    Pull it closer

THE OTHER

    I can't pull it any closer

THE ONE

    The keel's stuck on the bottom

THE OTHER

    Right

THE ONE

    Can you reach it

THE OTHER

    I'll try

    THE OTHER just manages to get hold of the gunwale and he jumps and crawls onto the deck, gets to his feet

    That was close

THE ONE

    I'll pull us out and haul anchor

    THE OTHER coils up the rope and puts it in the crate and THE ONE hauls the anchor

    I told you you could do it

THE OTHER

    Only just

THE ONE

    So

THE OTHER

    Where are we going

THE ONE

On a little ocean journey

I think

THE OTHER

The sea's calm

THE ONE

Fairly calm

But there's a nice gentle wind

THE OTHER

Don't take us too far out

THE ONE

I won't

quite short pause

of course I won't

THE OTHER

Just

a little way out

THE ONE

Yes

Pause. THE ONE stands with his hand on the tiller and THE OTHER stands next to him and looks forward

THE OTHER

The ocean's terrifying

THE ONE

Yes it is

THE OTHER

It fills up everything there is

THE ONE

But it's beautiful

the ocean's beautiful too

THE OTHER

Kind of

THE ONE

You don't think it's beautiful

THE OTHER

Its mostly frightening

short pause

but we don't need to go too far out do we

THE ONE

No

quite short pause

a bit further than this though

we'll have to venture a bit further out

THE OTHER

A little bit further

THE ONE

Yes

Long pause

THE OTHER

You're heading straight out to sea

THE ONE

I know

Pause

THE OTHER

Why

THE ONE

You may as well get out on the ocean

really

now that you're in the boat with me

now you're out on the water

THE OTHER

What if the wind picks up

With that fog out there

THE ONE

But the sea's really calm

The sky's so clear

Quite short pause

It's a good wind

THE OTHER

But it changes really quickly

on the ocean

THE ONE

It can do

quite short pause

yes

THE OTHER

Why don't we turn back

THE ONE

Not yet

quite short pause

a little bit further

quite short pause

we've got to go a bit further out

A little bit further

Long pause

THE OTHER

Can we turn back

please

Long pause

I'm getting a bit frightened

THE ONE

Right

Pause

I'll turn back

Long pause

THE OTHER

You're still heading straight out

you're steering

straight out to the ocean

Long pause

I'm getting frightened

quite short pause

I'm frightened

THE ONE

       Not seriously

THE OTHER

       I am

THE ONE

       You're not

       quite short pause

       this boat's so solid

       she's safe

       quite short pause

       the weather's perfect

       quite short pause

       there's a good wind

       quite short pause

       everything's fine

THE OTHER

       But I'm very frightened

THE ONE

       Me too

THE OTHER

       You too

THE ONE

       Yes

       Pause

THE OTHER

       Then why don't you turn back

       quite short pause

       why don't you

THE ONE

       Well

       THE ONE keeps heading straight for the open ocean. Long pause

THE OTHER

       Don't go any further

THE ONE

       I won't

THE OTHER

    Turn back then

    Long pause

    We've gone far enough now

    quite short pause

    stop messing around

    quite short pause

    turn back

    please

THE ONE

    Well

    quite short pause

    soon

    I'll turn back soon

THE OTHER

    Tell me what it was you wanted to say

    you said you wanted to say something to me

    what was it

THE ONE

    I didn't want to say anything

    I've not got anything to tell you

    Long pause

THE OTHER

    Tell me why you did it

THE ONE

    No I

    Short pause

    I

    breaks off. Pause

THE OTHER

    You

THE ONE

    I

    breaks off

THE OTHER

      Yes

      quite short pause

      say it

THE ONE

      I

      breaks off

      no it's nothing

THE OTHER

      Say it

      Pause

THE ONE

      I was always afraid that it was going to happen

      I thought it would happen

      I was terrified it would

THE OTHER

      Right

THE ONE

      And then it did

THE OTHER

      Yes

THE ONE

      It just happened

THE OTHER

      Yes

      Short pause

THE ONE

      There's nothing anybody can say about it

      Quite short pause

      And now I've gone

THE OTHER

      Short pause

      Why though

      quite short pause

      why did it happen

THE ONE

> There's no reason
> I knew it was going to happen
> And then it happened
> *Pause*

THE OTHER

> Right
> *Short pause*
> Why don't you turn back

THE ONE

> Well
> *quite short pause*
> Alright I'll turn back soon
> *Pause*

THE OTHER

> What happened

THE ONE

> I
> *breaks off*

THE OTHER

> No
> *Quite short pause*
> No don't say anything
> *Short pause*
> You
> *quite short pause*
> yes
> *quite short pause*
> yes when we'd come right out onto the ocean
> when we could only just make out the lighthouse
> way back there
> then
> *quite short pause*
> you remember
> you

THE ONE

> *Interrupts*
>
> Yes
>
> *Long pause*
>
> This is a good wind

THE OTHER

> Yes we're making good ground
>
> *Short pause*

THE ONE

> Why don't you take the tiller
>
> you

THE OTHER

> No I daren't

THE ONE

> Go on
>
> take it
>
> *THE OTHER takes the tiller*
>
> Just hold it steady
>
> hold this course
>
> *THE ONE goes out on the deck*

THE OTHER

> No don't stand there
>
> Not out here
>
> In the middle of the ocean
>
> Why are you doing that
>
> Why are you standing there
>
> Come on
>
> Sit back down
>
> *Quite short pause*
>
> The wind's picking up
>
> The waves are getting big
>
> I daren't do this
>
> We're closing in on the fog
>
> Take the tiller
>
> please

I'm frightened
Come on
Don't stand there
It's dangerous

THE ONE

It's not
quite short pause
it's fine
this

THE OTHER

Don't stand there
Come on
No don't do that
Come back
The waves are getting really big
Come back
I'm scared
Quite short pause
I don't want to steer the boat
You
take the boat
Quite short pause
Come back
Be careful
Please come back

THE ONE

I will be careful
Very long pause

THE OTHER

And then he stood there on the deck
He stood there and looked
quite short pause
and then
quite short pause
right then

then he sort of stumbled
quite short pause
and then he lay there in the sea
quite short pause
and I grabbed a life jacket
and I threw it to him
and the waves were huge
quite short pause
but he didn't reach for it
quite short pause
and the waves rolled over him
quite short pause
he was above the waves
quite short pause
he was under the waves
quite short pause
he lay there in the water
and the waves were getting bigger
quite short pause
I grabbed the boathook
I tried to reach him
I tried to get hold of him
but he pushed the boathook away
quite short pause
he was above the waves
quite short pause
he was under the waves
quite short pause
and then I saw him drift away behind the boat
quite short pause
and I
quite short pause
I had never sailed a boat before
I didn't know anything
In the middle of the ocean

the boat just drifts
the sails flapping
what am I meant to do
I pushed the tiller
nothing happened
the boat just kept drifting
and then
suddenly
the boat drifts forwards
but where is he
I look for him
I shout
where are you
he's nowhere to be seen
I've got to find him
I've got to get hold of him
the boat drifts forwards
I push the tiller
the boat stops
the sails flap
the boat lies there
and then it drifts backwards
and I look for him
I shout out
Where are you
the boat calms down
the sails flutter
I push the tiller
the boat drifts forwards
I look for him and look for him
I shout
Where are you
I shout again
Where are you
I look

The boat drifts forwards
I look and look
I push the tiller
the boat drifts forwards
I look and look
But I can't see him

THE ONE

I've gone

THE OTHER

I shout out
Where are you
The boat drifts forwards
I shout out
Where are you
The boat drifts forwards
I wait
I shout out
Where are you

THE ONE

I've gone

THE OTHER

I wait
The boat drifts forwards
I push the tiller
The boat drifts forwards
I've got to do something
Long pause
I look out over the water
quite short pause
and all I can see
is the open ocean
Everything's empty
Just ocean
Just sky
Just empty

just black
just white
and the waves
so big now the waves are
quite short pause
I look towards shore
quite short pause
and way back in there
quite short pause
way back in there I think I see the lighthouse
quite short pause
and now the waves smash against the boat
And I can't stay out here any more
I wait
I shout out
Where are you
The boat drifts forwards
I wait
I push the tiller
The boat drifts forwards
I hold the tiller steady
and the waves
the waves have become huge
black and white waves
and the sky is turning black
The ocean is black
I shout out
Where are you
I shout out
I don't know what to do
I look towards the lighthouse
I head towards the lighthouse
I look back
I shout out
Where are you

All I can see is the black sky

And the black ocean

And the black and white waves

And the boat dives down and climbs up

And the boat's up

then it's down

I see the lighthouse

I head towards the lighthouse

I hold the tiller steady

And the boat goes up and down

THE ONE

I've gone

THE OTHER

I shout out

Where are you

THE ONE

I'm not frightened anymore

I'm not heavy anymore

I'm only weight

and I'm not weight

I'm motion

I left with the wind

I am the wind

THE OTHER

I look towards the lighthouse

I shout out

Where are you

THE ONE

I've gone

THE OTHER

I shout

Where are you

THE ONE

I've gone now

THE OTHER

      And the boat moves up

      and down

      up

      and down

      and the waves

      the black waves

      the white waves

      quite short pause

      and then the rain

      And then it rains

      And the wind fills the sails

      And the boat rises up and up

      even higher

      and then falls down and down

      all the way down

      and then up

      quite short pause

      and I look towards the lighthouse

      I hold the tiller

      Long pause

THE ONE

      I've gone away now

      Long pause

THE OTHER

      But why did you do it

THE ONE

      I just did it

THE OTHER

      But you were so scared of doing it

THE ONE

      I was terrified of it

      And that's why I did it

      I knew I would

      Short pause

I was too heavy
quite short pause
and the sea was too light
And the wind moved so fast

THE OTHER

I thought it was just something you thought about
something you were afraid of

THE ONE

I did too
I thought it was like that too

THE OTHER

But then you did it

THE ONE

I know

THE OTHER

Why did you do it

THE ONE

I just did
Quite short pause
We were in the boat
And I just did it
Quite short pause
I did it because I was so heavy

THE OTHER

You did it

THE ONE

I've left

THE OTHER

You did it

THE ONE

I did it

THE OTHER

And you did it
right
because
breaks off

93

THE ONE

      I've gone now

      I left with the wind

THE OTHER

      You've gone now

THE ONE

      I've gone

      I left with the wind

      I am the wind

WWW.OBERONBOOKS.COM

Printed in the USA
CPSIA information can be obtained
at www.ICGtesting.com
LVHW050219011123
762635LV00005B/442